Daily Gratitude Journal for Kids

100 Days of Gratitude for a Super Awesome & Amazing Life

This Book Belongs to:

_____

Daily Gratitude Journal for Kids by Gratitude Daily
Published by Creative Ideas Publishing

© 2020 Gratitude Daily

All rights reserved. No portion of this book may be reproduced in any form without permission from the author, except as permitted by U.S. copyright law.

For permissions contact:
permissions@creativeideaspublishing.com

ISBN: 978-1-952016-11-0

How to Use

Dear Super Awesome and Amazing Friend,

Taking the time to fill out this journal each day will be so great for you and it is our hope that it will help "blast" your life into outer space and make everyday Super Awesome and Amazing!

If you miss a day, don't worry or be sad! Just do it the next day.

To the right is an example day that we already filled in. You can be thankful for "big things" like family and friends or you can be thankful for "small things" like a sunny day.

We believe you can almost always choose if you will have a Super Awesome and Amazing day or just an OK day. Decide what kind of day you will have and put a check mark next to your choice.

In the box, draw something that makes you happy or just draw something silly. Have fun with it!

Lastly, write something that you look forward to doing. Just like before, this can be a tiny thing or a big thing. Just be excited about something. (:

We believe in you! You are so smart and strong already that we are excited to see how Super Awesome and Amazing you will be after practicing daily gratitude for 100 days. Best of luck!

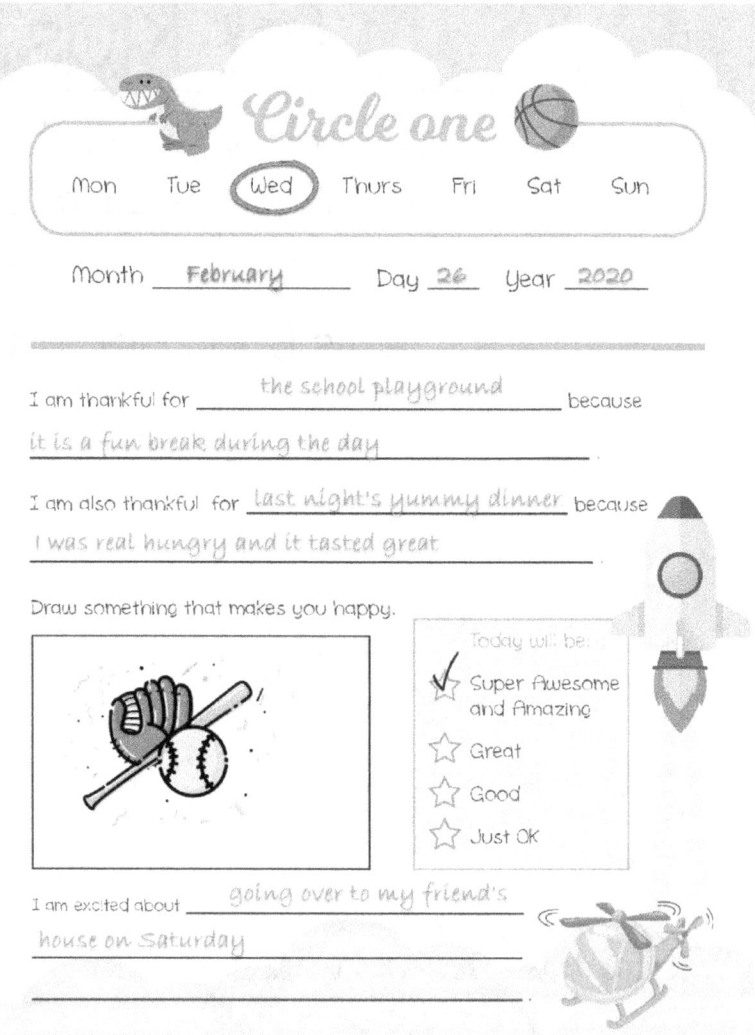

Daily Gratitude Journal for Kids

Circle one

Mon   Tue   Wed   Thurs   Fri   Sat   Sun

Month _____ Day _____ Year _____

I am thankful for _____ because

_____ .

I am also thankful for _____ because

_____ .

Draw something that makes you happy.

Today will be:

☆ Super Awesome and Amazing

☆ Great

☆ Good

☆ Just OK

I am excited about _____

_____

_____ .

Daily Gratitude Journal for Kids

 # Circle one

Mon   Tue   Wed   Thurs   Fri   Sat   Sun

Month _____   Day ____   Year _____

I am thankful for _____ because
_____ .

I am also thankful for _____ because
_____ .

Draw something that makes you happy.

Today will be:
☆ Super Awesome and Amazing
☆ Great
☆ Good
☆ Just OK

I am excited about _____
_____
_____

 # Circle one

Mon   Tue   Wed   Thurs   Fri   Sat   Sun

Month _____   Day ____   Year _____

I am thankful for _____ because
_____.

I am also thankful for _____ because
_____.

Draw something that makes you happy.

Today will be:
☆ Super Awesome and Amazing
☆ Great
☆ Good
☆ Just OK

I am excited about _____
_____.

 # Circle one

Mon   Tue   Wed   Thurs   Fri   Sat   Sun

Month _____ Day ____ Year _____

I am thankful for _____ because
_____ .

I am also thankful for _____ because
_____ .

Draw something that makes you happy.

Today will be:
☆ Super Awesome and Amazing
☆ Great
☆ Good
☆ Just Ok

I am excited about _____
_____
_____ .

Circle one

Mon   Tue   Wed   Thurs   Fri   Sat   Sun

Month _____ Day _____ Year _____

I am thankful for _____ because
_____ .

I am also thankful for _____ because
_____ .

Draw something that makes you happy.

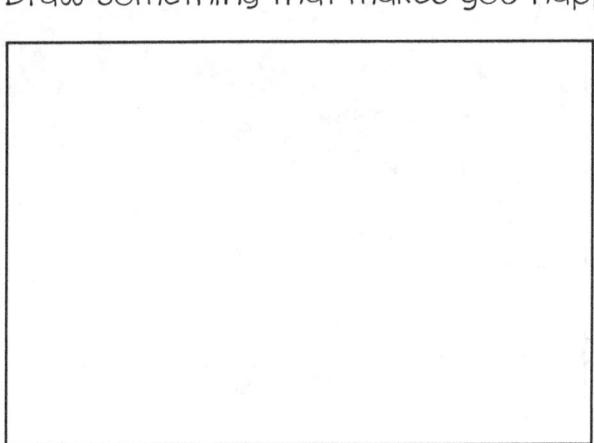

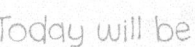

☆ Super Awesome and Amazing
☆ Great
☆ Good
☆ Just OK

I am excited about _____
_____ .

Daily Gratitude Journal for Kids

Circle one

Mon   Tue   Wed   Thurs   Fri   Sat   Sun

Month _____   Day ____   Year _____

I am thankful for _____ because
_____ .

I am also thankful for _____ because
_____ .

Draw something that makes you happy.

Today will be:
☆ Super Awesome and Amazing
☆ Great
☆ Good
☆ Just OK

I am excited about _____
_____
_____ .

Circle one

Mon   Tue   Wed   Thurs   Fri   Sat   Sun

Month _____ Day ____ Year _____

I am thankful for _____ because
_____ .

I am also thankful for _____ because
_____ .

Draw something that makes you happy.

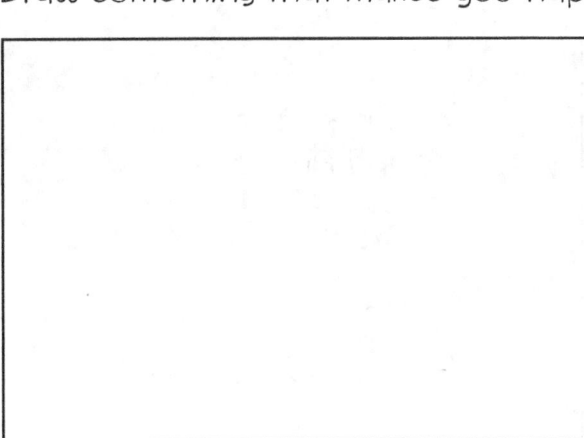

Today will be:

 Super Awesome and Amazing

 Great

 Good

 Just OK

I am excited about _____
_____
_____ .

 **Circle one**

Mon   Tue   Wed   Thurs   Fri   Sat   Sun

Month _____ Day _____ Year _____

I am thankful for _____ because

_____ .

I am also thankful for _____ because

_____ .

Draw something that makes you happy.

Today will be:
 Super Awesome and Amazing
 Great
 Good
 Just Ok

I am excited about _____

_____

_____ .

Daily Gratitude Journal for Kids

Circle one

Mon   Tue   Wed   Thurs   Fri   Sat   Sun

Month _____   Day ____   Year _____

I am thankful for _____ because _____ .

I am also thankful for _____ because _____ .

Draw something that makes you happy.

Today will be:
- ☆ Super Awesome and Amazing
- ☆ Great
- ☆ Good
- ☆ Just OK

I am excited about _____
_____ .

Daily Gratitude Journal for Kids

Circle one

Mon   Tue   Wed   Thurs   Fri   Sat   Sun

Month _____   Day ____   Year _____

I am thankful for _____ because
_____ .

I am also thankful for _____ because
_____ .

Draw something that makes you happy.

Today will be:
☆ Super Awesome and Amazing
☆ Great
☆ Good
☆ Just Ok

I am excited about _____
_____
_____ .

Circle one

Mon   Tue   Wed   Thurs   Fri   Sat   Sun

Month _____   Day ____   Year _____

I am thankful for _____ because
_____ .

I am also thankful for _____ because
_____ .

Draw something that makes you happy.

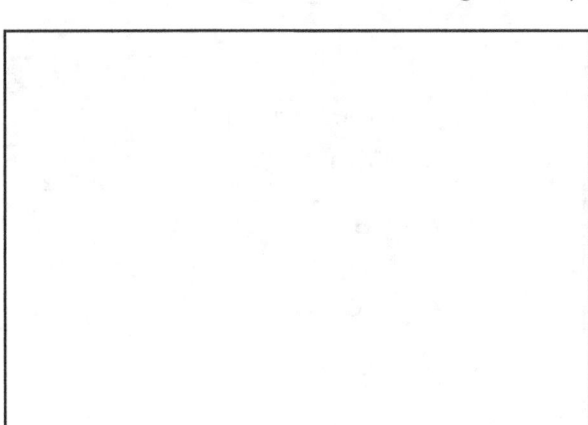

Today will be:

 Super Awesome and Amazing

 Great

 Good

 Just OK

I am excited about _____
_____
_____ .

Daily Gratitude Journal for Kids

Circle one

Mon   Tue   Wed   Thurs   Fri   Sat   Sun

Month _____ Day ____ Year _____

I am thankful for _____ because _____ .

I am also thankful for _____ because _____ .

Draw something that makes you happy.

 Today will be:

 Super Awesome and Amazing

 Great

 Good

 Just OK

I am excited about _____ .

Daily Gratitude Journal for Kids

Circle one

Mon   Tue   Wed   Thurs   Fri   Sat   Sun

Month _____ Day ____ Year _____

I am thankful for _____ because
_____ .

I am also thankful for _____ because
_____ .

Draw something that makes you happy.

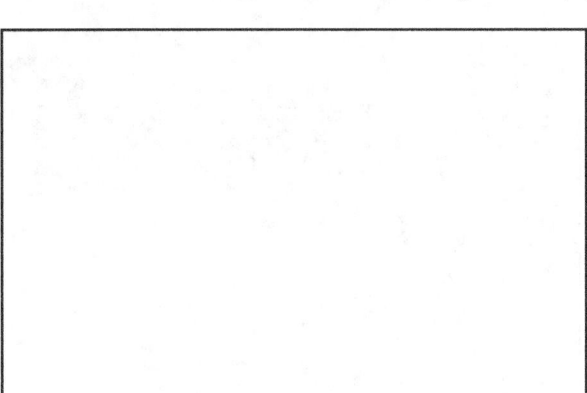

Today will be:
 Super Awesome and Amazing
 Great
 Good
 Just OK

I am excited about _____
_____
_____ .

Daily Gratitude Journal for Kids

Circle one

Mon   Tue   Wed   Thurs   Fri   Sat   Sun

Month _____ Day _____ Year _____

I am thankful for _____ because

_____ .

I am also thankful for _____ because

_____ .

Draw something that makes you happy.

Today will be:
- ☆ Super Awesome and Amazing
- ☆ Great
- ☆ Good
- ☆ Just OK

I am excited about _____

_____

_____ .

 # Circle one

Mon   Tue   Wed   Thurs   Fri   Sat   Sun

Month _____ Day ____ Year _____

I am thankful for _____ because
_____ .

I am also thankful for _____ because
_____ .

Draw something that makes you happy.

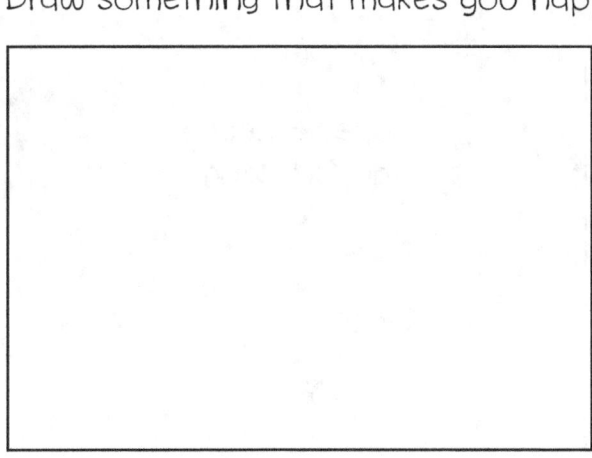

Today will be:

 Super Awesome and Amazing

 Great

 Good

 Just OK

I am excited about _____
_____
_____ .

 **Circle one**

Mon   Tue   Wed   Thurs   Fri   Sat   Sun

Month _____ Day ____ Year _____

I am thankful for _____ because

_____ .

I am also thankful for _____ because

_____ .

Draw something that makes you happy.

Today will be:
☆ Super Awesome and Amazing
☆ Great
☆ Good
☆ Just Ok

I am excited about _____

_____

_____ .

Circle one

Mon   Tue   Wed   Thurs   Fri   Sat   Sun

Month _____ Day ____ Year _____

I am thankful for _____ because
_____ .

I am also thankful for _____ because
_____ .

Draw something that makes you happy.

Today will be:
- ☆ Super Awesome and Amazing
- ☆ Great
- ☆ Good
- ☆ Just OK

I am excited about _____
_____ .

 # Circle one

Mon   Tue   Wed   Thurs   Fri   Sat   Sun

Month _____   Day ____   Year _____

I am thankful for _____ because
_____ .

I am also thankful for _____ because
_____ .

Draw something that makes you happy.

Today will be:
☆ Super Awesome and Amazing
☆ Great
☆ Good
☆ Just Ok

I am excited about _____
_____
_____ .

Circle one

Mon   Tue   Wed   Thurs   Fri   Sat   Sun

Month _____ Day ____ Year _____

I am thankful for _____ because

_____ .

I am also thankful for _____ because

_____ .

Draw something that makes you happy.

Today will be:

 Super Awesome and Amazing

 Great

 Good

 Just OK

I am excited about _____

_____

_____ .

Daily Gratitude Journal for Kids

Circle one

Mon   Tue   Wed   Thurs   Fri   Sat   Sun

Month _____   Day ____   Year _____

I am thankful for _____ because

_____ .

I am also thankful for _____ because

_____ .

Draw something that makes you happy.

Today will be:
- ☆ Super Awesome and Amazing
- ☆ Great
- ☆ Good
- ☆ Just Ok

I am excited about _____

_____

_____ .

Daily Gratitude Journal for Kids

 # Circle one

Mon   Tue   Wed   Thurs   Fri   Sat   Sun

Month _____   Day _____   Year _____

I am thankful for _____ because

_____ .

I am also thankful for _____ because

_____ .

Draw something that makes you happy.

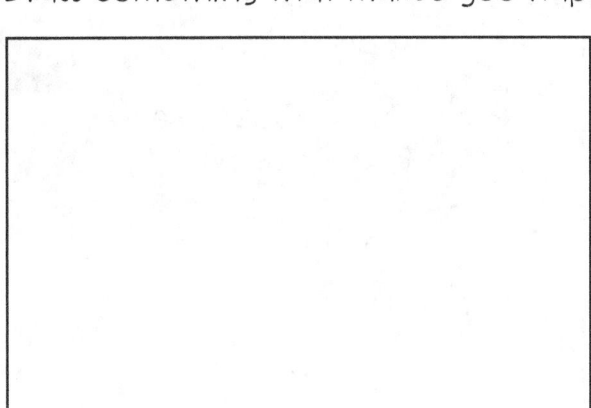

Today will be:

 Super Awesome and Amazing

 Great

 Good

 Just OK

I am excited about _____

_____

_____ .

Daily Gratitude Journal for Kids

Circle one

Mon   Tue   Wed   Thurs   Fri   Sat   Sun

Month _____ Day ____ Year _____

I am thankful for _____ because _____ .

I am also thankful for _____ because _____ .

Draw something that makes you happy.

Today will be:
☆ Super Awesome and Amazing
☆ Great
☆ Good
☆ Just OK

I am excited about _____
_____
_____ .

 # Circle one

Mon Tue Wed Thurs Fri Sat Sun

Month _____ Day _____ Year _____

I am thankful for _____ because
_____ .

I am also thankful for _____ because
_____ .

Draw something that makes you happy.

Today will be:

 Super Awesome and Amazing

 Great

 Good

 Just Ok

I am excited about _____
_____
_____ .

Daily Gratitude Journal for Kids

Circle one

Mon Tue Wed Thurs Fri Sat Sun

Month _____ Day ____ Year _____

I am thankful for _____ because

_____ .

I am also thankful for _____ because

_____ .

Draw something that makes you happy.

Today will be:
- ☆ Super Awesome and Amazing
- ☆ Great
- ☆ Good
- ☆ Just OK

I am excited about _____

_____

_____ .

Circle one

Mon   Tue   Wed   Thurs   Fri   Sat   Sun

Month _____   Day _____   Year _____

I am thankful for _____ because
_____ .

I am also thankful for _____ because
_____ .

Draw something that makes you happy.

Today will be:

 Super Awesome and Amazing

 Great

 Good

 Just OK

I am excited about _____
_____
_____ .

Daily Gratitude Journal for Kids

 **Circle one**

Mon   Tue   Wed   Thurs   Fri   Sat   Sun

Month _____   Day ____   Year _____

I am thankful for _____ because _____ .

I am also thankful for _____ because _____ .

Draw something that makes you happy.

Today will be:
☆ Super Awesome and Amazing
☆ Great
☆ Good
☆ Just OK

I am excited about _____
_____
_____ .

 # Circle one

Mon   Tue   Wed   Thurs   Fri   Sat   Sun

Month _____ Day ____ Year _____

I am thankful for _____ because
_____.

I am also thankful for _____ because
_____.

Draw something that makes you happy.

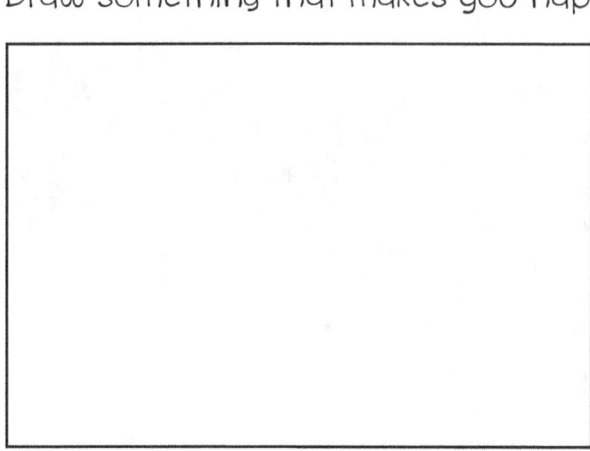

Today will be:
 Super Awesome and Amazing
 Great
 Good
 Just OK

I am excited about _____
_____
_____.

Daily Gratitude Journal for Kids

Circle one

Mon   Tue   Wed   Thurs   Fri   Sat   Sun

Month _____   Day ____   Year _____

I am thankful for _____ because

_____ .

I am also thankful for _____ because

_____ .

Draw something that makes you happy.

Today will be:
- ☆ Super Awesome and Amazing
- ☆ Great
- ☆ Good
- ☆ Just OK

I am excited about _____

_____

_____ .

Circle one

Mon   Tue   Wed   Thurs   Fri   Sat   Sun

Month _____ Day ____ Year _____

I am thankful for _____ because
_____ .

I am also thankful for _____ because
_____ .

Draw something that makes you happy.

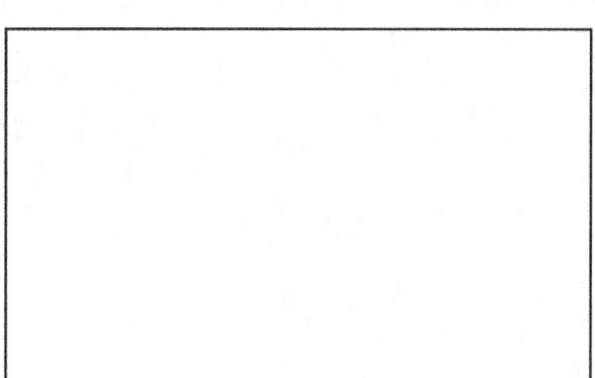

Today will be:

 Super Awesome and Amazing

 Great

 Good

 Just OK

I am excited about _____
_____
_____ .

Daily Gratitude Journal for Kids

 **Circle one**

Mon   Tue   Wed   Thurs   Fri   Sat   Sun

Month _____ Day ____ Year _____

I am thankful for _____ because
_____ .

I am also thankful for _____ because
_____ .

Draw something that makes you happy.

Today will be:
☆ Super Awesome and Amazing
☆ Great
☆ Good
☆ Just OK

I am excited about _____
_____
_____ .

 # Circle one

Mon   Tue   Wed   Thurs   Fri   Sat   Sun

Month _____ Day _____ Year _____

I am thankful for _____ because
_____ .

I am also thankful for _____ because
_____ .

Draw something that makes you happy.

Today will be:
 Super Awesome and Amazing
 Great
 Good
 Just OK

I am excited about _____
_____
_____ .

Circle one

Mon   Tue   Wed   Thurs   Fri   Sat   Sun

Month _____   Day ____   Year _____

I am thankful for _____ because
_____ .

I am also thankful for _____ because
_____ .

Draw something that makes you happy.

Today will be:
☆ Super Awesome and Amazing
☆ Great
☆ Good
☆ Just OK

I am excited about _____
_____
_____ .

 # Circle one

Mon   Tue   Wed   Thurs   Fri   Sat   Sun

Month _____ Day _____ Year _____

I am thankful for _____ because
_____ .

I am also thankful for _____ because
_____ .

Draw something that makes you happy.

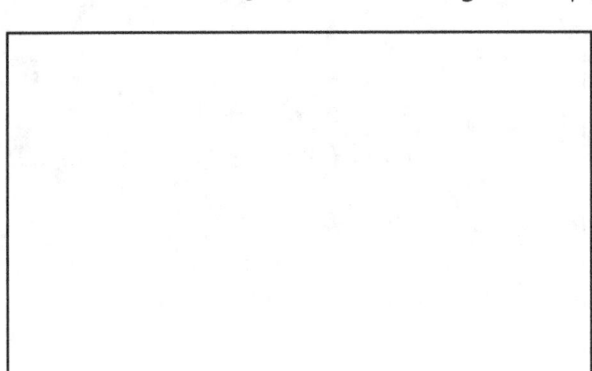

Today will be:

 Super Awesome and Amazing

 Great

 Good

 Just OK

I am excited about _____
_____
_____ .

Circle one

Mon   Tue   Wed   Thurs   Fri   Sat   Sun

Month _____ Day ____ Year _____

I am thankful for _____ because
_____ .

I am also thankful for _____ because
_____ .

Draw something that makes you happy.

[drawing box]

Today will be:
☆ Super Awesome and Amazing
☆ Great
☆ Good
☆ Just OK

I am excited about _____
_____
_____ .

Circle one

Mon   Tue   Wed   Thurs   Fri   Sat   Sun

Month _____ Day _____ Year _____

I am thankful for _____ because

_____ .

I am also thankful for _____ because

_____ .

Draw something that makes you happy.

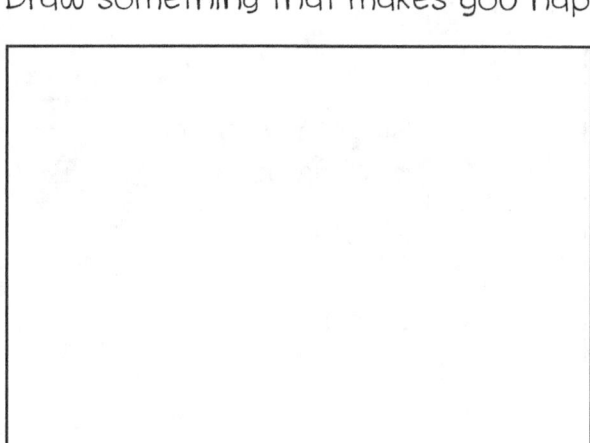

Today will be:

 Super Awesome and Amazing

 Great

 Good

 Just OK

I am excited about _____

_____

_____ .

Daily Gratitude Journal for Kids

Circle one

Mon   Tue   Wed   Thurs   Fri   Sat   Sun

Month _____   Day ____   Year _____

I am thankful for _____ because
_____ .

I am also thankful for _____ because
_____ .

Draw something that makes you happy.

Today will be:
☆ Super Awesome and Amazing
☆ Great
☆ Good
☆ Just OK

I am excited about _____
_____
_____ .

Circle one

Mon   Tue   Wed   Thurs   Fri   Sat   Sun

Month _____   Day ____   Year _____

I am thankful for _____ because
_____ .

I am also thankful for _____ because
_____ .

Draw something that makes you happy.

Today will be:

 Super Awesome and Amazing

 Great

 Good

 Just OK

I am excited about _____
_____
_____ .

 **Circle one**

Mon   Tue   Wed   Thurs   Fri   Sat   Sun

Month _____ Day _____ Year _____

I am thankful for _____ because
_____ .

I am also thankful for _____ because
_____ .

Draw something that makes you happy.

Today will be:
☆ Super Awesome and Amazing
☆ Great
☆ Good
☆ Just OK

I am excited about _____
_____
_____ .

38   Daily Gratitude Journal for Kids

Circle one

Mon   Tue   Wed   Thurs   Fri   Sat   Sun

Month _____ Day ____ Year _____

I am thankful for _____ because
_____ .

I am also thankful for _____ because
_____ .

Draw something that makes you happy.

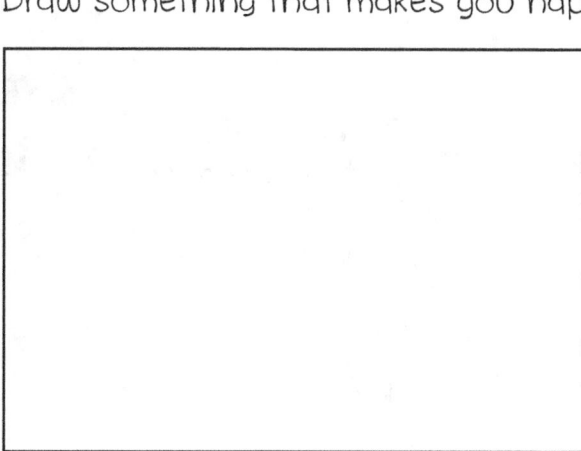

Today will be:

 Super Awesome and Amazing

 Great

 Good

 Just OK

I am excited about _____
_____
_____ .

Daily Gratitude Journal for Kids

 **Circle one**

Mon   Tue   Wed   Thurs   Fri   Sat   Sun

Month _____   Day ____   Year _____

I am thankful for _____ because
_____ .

I am also thankful for _____ because
_____ .

Draw something that makes you happy.

Today will be:
☆ Super Awesome and Amazing
☆ Great
☆ Good
☆ Just OK

I am excited about _____
_____
_____

 # Circle one

Mon   Tue   Wed   Thurs   Fri   Sat   Sun

Month _____ Day ____ Year _____

I am thankful for _____ because _____ .

I am also thankful for _____ because _____ .

Draw something that makes you happy.

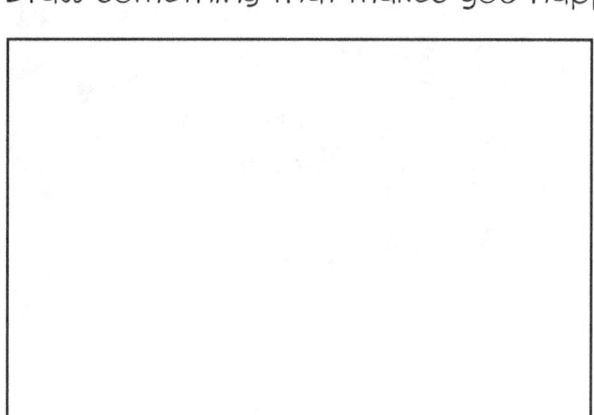

Today will be:

 Super Awesome and Amazing

 Great

 Good

 Just OK

I am excited about _____
_____
_____ .

Daily Gratitude Journal for Kids

Circle one

Mon   Tue   Wed   Thurs   Fri   Sat   Sun

Month _____ Day ____ Year _____

I am thankful for _____ because
_____ .

I am also thankful for _____ because
_____ .

Draw something that makes you happy.

Today will be:
☆ Super Awesome and Amazing
☆ Great
☆ Good
☆ Just OK

I am excited about _____
_____
_____ .

Circle one

Mon   Tue   Wed   Thurs   Fri   Sat   Sun

Month _____ Day ____ Year _____

I am thankful for _____ because

_____ .

I am also thankful for _____ because

_____ .

Draw something that makes you happy.

Today will be:

 Super Awesome and Amazing

 Great

 Good

 Just OK

I am excited about _____

_____

_____ .

Daily Gratitude Journal for Kids

 **Circle one**

Mon   Tue   Wed   Thurs   Fri   Sat   Sun

Month _____ Day ____ Year _____

I am thankful for _____ because
_____ .

I am also thankful for _____ because
_____ .

Draw something that makes you happy.

Today will be:
- ☆ Super Awesome and Amazing
- ☆ Great
- ☆ Good
- ☆ Just OK

I am excited about _____
_____
_____ .

Daily Gratitude Journal for Kids

Circle one

Mon   Tue   Wed   Thurs   Fri   Sat   Sun

Month _____ Day ____ Year _____

I am thankful for _____ because
_____ .

I am also thankful for _____ because
_____ .

Draw something that makes you happy.

Today will be:
- ☆ Super Awesome and Amazing
- ☆ Great
- ☆ Good
- ☆ Just OK

I am excited about _____
_____
_____ .

Daily Gratitude Journal for Kids

Circle one

Mon   Tue   Wed   Thurs   Fri   Sat   Sun

Month _____ Day ____ Year _____

I am thankful for _____ because

_____ .

I am also thankful for _____ because

_____ .

Draw something that makes you happy.

Today will be:
- ☆ Super Awesome and Amazing
- ☆ Great
- ☆ Good
- ☆ Just OK

I am excited about _____

_____

_____ .

Circle one

Mon   Tue   Wed   Thurs   Fri   Sat   Sun

Month _____ Day ____ Year _____

I am thankful for _____ because
_____ .

I am also thankful for _____ because
_____ .

Draw something that makes you happy.

Today will be:
- ☆ Super Awesome and Amazing
- ☆ Great
- ☆ Good
- ☆ Just OK

I am excited about _____
_____
_____ .

Daily Gratitude Journal for Kids

Circle one

Mon   Tue   Wed   Thurs   Fri   Sat   Sun

Month _____   Day ____   Year _____

I am thankful for _____ because
_____ .

I am also thankful for _____ because
_____ .

Draw something that makes you happy.

Today will be:
☆ Super Awesome and Amazing
☆ Great
☆ Good
☆ Just OK

I am excited about _____
_____
_____ .

Circle one

Mon   Tue   Wed   Thurs   Fri   Sat   Sun

Month _____ Day ____ Year _____

I am thankful for _____ because
_____ .

I am also thankful for _____ because
_____ .

Draw something that makes you happy.

Today will be:
☆ Super Awesome and Amazing
☆ Great
☆ Good
☆ Just OK

I am excited about _____
_____
_____ .

Daily Gratitude Journal for Kids

Circle one

Mon   Tue   Wed   Thurs   Fri   Sat   Sun

Month _____ Day ____ Year _____

I am thankful for _____ because
_____ .

I am also thankful for _____ because
_____ .

Draw something that makes you happy.

Today will be:
☆ Super Awesome and Amazing
☆ Great
☆ Good
☆ Just OK

I am excited about _____
_____
_____ .

Circle one

Mon   Tue   Wed   Thurs   Fri   Sat   Sun

Month _____   Day _____   Year _____

I am thankful for _____ because

_____ .

I am also thankful for _____ because

_____ .

Draw something that makes you happy.

Today will be:
- ☆ Super Awesome and Amazing
- ☆ Great
- ☆ Good
- ☆ Just OK

I am excited about _____

_____

_____ .

 **Circle one**

Mon   Tue   Wed   Thurs   Fri   Sat   Sun

Month _____ Day ____ Year _____

I am thankful for _____ because
_____ .

I am also thankful for _____ because
_____ .

Draw something that makes you happy.

Today will be:
☆ Super Awesome and Amazing
☆ Great
☆ Good
☆ Just OK

I am excited about _____
_____
_____ .

Circle one

Mon   Tue   Wed   Thurs   Fri   Sat   Sun

Month _____   Day _____   Year _____

I am thankful for _____ because

_____ .

I am also thankful for _____ because

_____ .

Draw something that makes you happy.

Today will be:
- ☆ Super Awesome and Amazing
- ☆ Great
- ☆ Good
- ☆ Just OK

I am excited about _____

_____

_____ .

Daily Gratitude Journal for Kids   53

Circle one

Mon   Tue   Wed   Thurs   Fri   Sat   Sun

Month _____   Day ____   Year _____

I am thankful for _____ because
_____ .

I am also thankful for _____ because
_____ .

Draw something that makes you happy.

Today will be:
☆ Super Awesome and Amazing
☆ Great
☆ Good
☆ Just OK

I am excited about _____
_____
_____ .

Circle one

Mon   Tue   Wed   Thurs   Fri   Sat   Sun

Month _____   Day ____   Year _____

I am thankful for _____ because

_____ .

I am also thankful for _____ because

_____ .

Draw something that makes you happy.

Today will be:

 Super Awesome and Amazing

 Great

 Good

 Just OK

I am excited about _____

_____

_____ .

Daily Gratitude Journal for Kids

 # Circle one

Mon   Tue   Wed   Thurs   Fri   Sat   Sun

Month _____ Day ____ Year _____

I am thankful for _____ because _____ .

I am also thankful for _____ because _____ .

Draw something that makes you happy.

Today will be:

 Super Awesome and Amazing

 Great

 Good

 Just Ok

I am excited about _____
_____
_____ .

Daily Gratitude Journal for Kids

 # Circle one

Mon   Tue   Wed   Thurs   Fri   Sat   Sun

Month _____ Day ____ Year _____

I am thankful for _____ because
_____ .

I am also thankful for _____ because
_____ .

Draw something that makes you happy.

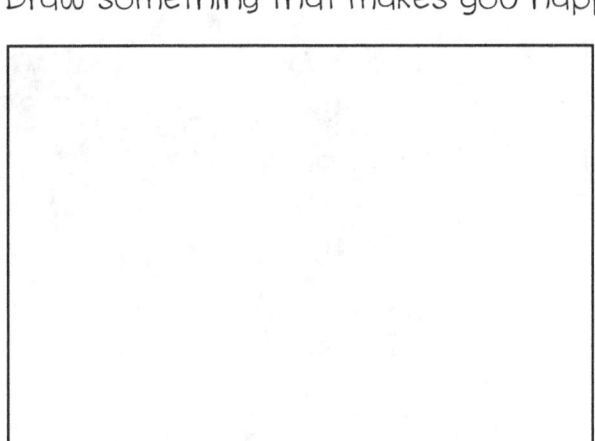

Today will be:
- Super Awesome and Amazing
- Great
- Good
- Just OK

I am excited about _____
_____
_____ .

 **Circle one**

Mon   Tue   Wed   Thurs   Fri   Sat   Sun

Month _____   Day ____   Year _____

I am thankful for _____ because
_____ .

I am also thankful for _____ because
_____ .

Draw something that makes you happy.

Today will be:
☆ Super Awesome and Amazing
☆ Great
☆ Good
☆ Just OK

I am excited about _____
_____
_____ .

Circle one

Mon   Tue   Wed   Thurs   Fri   Sat   Sun

Month _____ Day ____ Year _____

I am thankful for _____ because
_____ .

I am also thankful for _____ because
_____ .

Draw something that makes you happy.

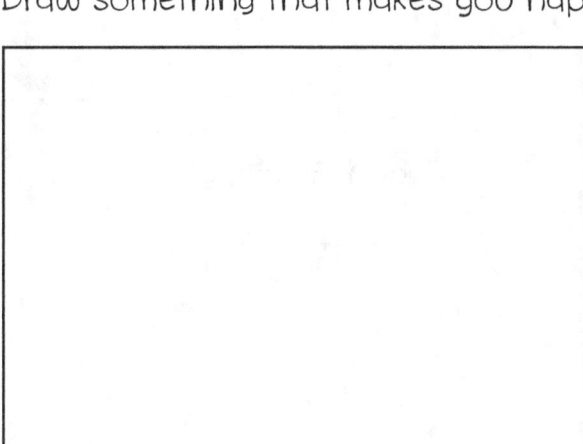

Today will be:
- ☆ Super Awesome and Amazing
- ☆ Great
- ☆ Good
- ☆ Just OK

I am excited about _____
_____
_____ .

Circle one

Mon   Tue   Wed   Thurs   Fri   Sat   Sun

Month _____   Day ____   Year _____

I am thankful for _____ because
_____ .

I am also thankful for _____ because
_____ .

Draw something that makes you happy.

Today will be:
☆ Super Awesome and Amazing
☆ Great
☆ Good
☆ Just OK

I am excited about _____
_____
_____

Circle one

Mon   Tue   Wed   Thurs   Fri   Sat   Sun

Month _____ Day ____ Year _____

I am thankful for _____ because
_____ .

I am also thankful for _____ because
_____ .

Draw something that makes you happy.

Today will be:
☆ Super Awesome and Amazing
☆ Great
☆ Good
☆ Just OK

I am excited about _____
_____ .

Circle one

Mon   Tue   Wed   Thurs   Fri   Sat   Sun

Month _____ Day _____ Year _____

I am thankful for _____ because
_____ .

I am also thankful for _____ because
_____ .

Draw something that makes you happy.

Today will be:
- ☆ Super Awesome and Amazing
- ☆ Great
- ☆ Good
- ☆ Just OK

I am excited about _____
_____
_____ .

Circle one

Mon   Tue   Wed   Thurs   Fri   Sat   Sun

Month _____ Day ____ Year _____

I am thankful for _____ because
_____ .

I am also thankful for _____ because
_____ .

Draw something that makes you happy.

Today will be:
☆ Super Awesome and Amazing
☆ Great
☆ Good
☆ Just OK

I am excited about _____
_____
_____ .

 # Circle one

Mon   Tue   Wed   Thurs   Fri   Sat   Sun

Month _____ Day ____ Year _____

I am thankful for _____ because
_____ .

I am also thankful for _____ because
_____ .

Draw something that makes you happy.

Today will be:
☆ Super Awesome and Amazing
☆ Great
☆ Good
☆ Just OK

I am excited about _____
_____
_____ .

Circle one

Mon   Tue   Wed   Thurs   Fri   Sat   Sun

Month _____   Day ____   Year _____

I am thankful for _____ because
_____ .

I am also thankful for _____ because
_____ .

Draw something that makes you happy.

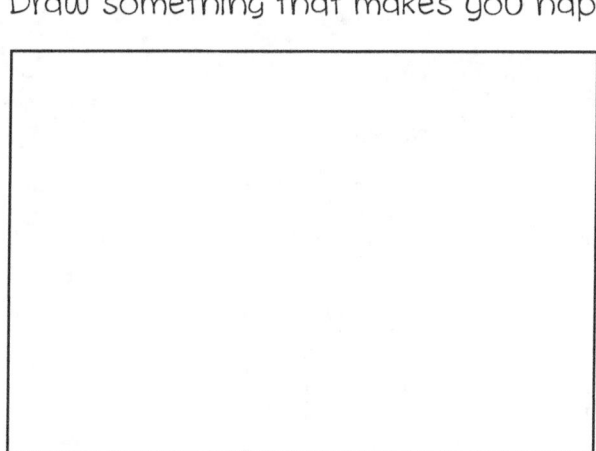

Today will be:

 Super Awesome and Amazing

 Great

 Good

 Just OK

I am excited about _____
_____
_____ .

Daily Gratitude Journal for Kids

Circle one

Mon   Tue   Wed   Thurs   Fri   Sat   Sun

Month _____ Day ____ Year _____

I am thankful for _____ because
_____ .

I am also thankful for _____ because
_____ .

Draw something that makes you happy.

Today will be:
☆ Super Awesome and Amazing
☆ Great
☆ Good
☆ Just Ok

I am excited about _____
_____
_____ .

Circle one

Mon   Tue   Wed   Thurs   Fri   Sat   Sun

Month _____ Day ____ Year _____

I am thankful for _____ because
_____ .

I am also thankful for _____ because
_____ .

Draw something that makes you happy.

Today will be:
- ☆ Super Awesome and Amazing
- ☆ Great
- ☆ Good
- ☆ Just OK

I am excited about _____
_____
_____ .

Daily Gratitude Journal for Kids

 **Circle one**

Mon   Tue   Wed   Thurs   Fri   Sat   Sun

Month _____   Day ____   Year _____

I am thankful for _____ because
_____ .

I am also thankful for _____ because
_____ .

Draw something that makes you happy.

Today will be:
☆ Super Awesome and Amazing
☆ Great
☆ Good
☆ Just OK

I am excited about _____
_____
_____

Circle one

Mon　　Tue　　Wed　　Thurs　　Fri　　Sat　　Sun

Month _____　Day ____　Year _____

I am thankful for _____ because
_____ .

I am also thankful for _____ because
_____ .

Draw something that makes you happy.

Today will be:
☆ Super Awesome and Amazing
☆ Great
☆ Good
☆ Just OK

I am excited about _____
_____
_____ .

Circle one

Mon   Tue   Wed   Thurs   Fri   Sat   Sun

Month _____ Day ____ Year _____

I am thankful for _____ because
_____ .

I am also thankful for _____ because
_____ .

Draw something that makes you happy.

Today will be:
☆ Super Awesome and Amazing
☆ Great
☆ Good
☆ Just Ok

I am excited about _____
_____
_____ .

Circle one

Mon   Tue   Wed   Thurs   Fri   Sat   Sun

Month _____ Day _____ Year _____

I am thankful for _____ because
_____ .

I am also thankful for _____ because
_____ .

Draw something that makes you happy.

Today will be:

 Super Awesome and Amazing

 Great

 Good

 Just OK

I am excited about _____
_____
_____ .

Daily Gratitude Journal for Kids

 **Circle one**

Mon   Tue   Wed   Thurs   Fri   Sat   Sun

Month _____   Day ____   Year _____

I am thankful for _____ because
_____ .

I am also thankful for _____ because
_____ .

Draw something that makes you happy.

Today will be:
☆ Super Awesome and Amazing
☆ Great
☆ Good
☆ Just OK

I am excited about _____
_____
_____

Circle one

Mon   Tue   Wed   Thurs   Fri   Sat   Sun

Month _____ Day _____ Year _____

I am thankful for _____ because
_____ .

I am also thankful for _____ because
_____ .

Draw something that makes you happy.

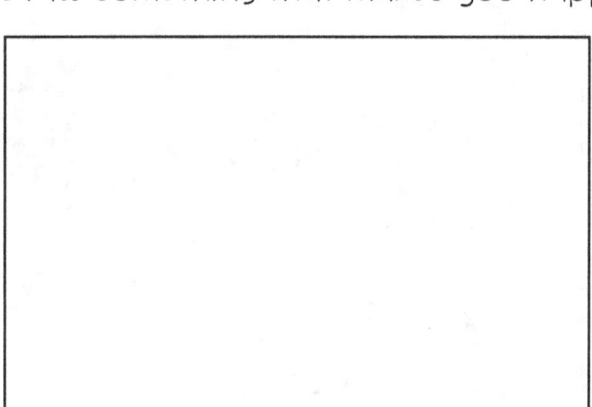

Today will be:
- ☆ Super Awesome and Amazing
- ☆ Great
- ☆ Good
- ☆ Just OK

I am excited about _____
_____
_____ .

Daily Gratitude Journal for Kids

 **Circle one**

Mon   Tue   Wed   Thurs   Fri   Sat   Sun

Month _____   Day ____   Year _____

I am thankful for _____ because
_____ .

I am also thankful for _____ because
_____ .

Draw something that makes you happy.

Today will be:
 Super Awesome and Amazing
 Great
 Good
 Just OK

I am excited about _____
_____
_____ .

Circle one

Mon   Tue   Wed   Thurs   Fri   Sat   Sun

Month _____ Day ____ Year _____

I am thankful for _____ because
_____ .

I am also thankful for _____ because
_____ .

Draw something that makes you happy.

Today will be:
 Super Awesome and Amazing
 Great
 Good
 Just OK

I am excited about _____
_____
_____ .

Daily Gratitude Journal for Kids

 # Circle one

Mon   Tue   Wed   Thurs   Fri   Sat   Sun

Month _____ Day ____ Year _____

I am thankful for _____ because

_____ .

I am also thankful for _____ because

_____ .

Draw something that makes you happy.

Today will be:
☆ Super Awesome and Amazing
☆ Great
☆ Good
☆ Just OK

I am excited about _____

_____

_____ .

 **Circle one**

Mon   Tue   Wed   Thurs   Fri   Sat   Sun

Month _____ Day ____ Year _____

I am thankful for _____ because _____.

I am also thankful for _____ because _____.

Draw something that makes you happy.

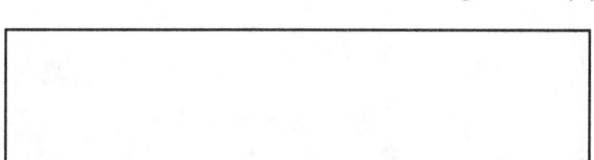

Today will be:
☆ Super Awesome and Amazing
☆ Great
☆ Good
☆ Just OK

I am excited about _____
_____
_____.

Circle one

Mon   Tue   Wed   Thurs   Fri   Sat   Sun

Month _____ Day ____ Year _____

I am thankful for _____ because

_____ .

I am also thankful for _____ because

_____ .

Draw something that makes you happy.

Today will be:
- ☆ Super Awesome and Amazing
- ☆ Great
- ☆ Good
- ☆ Just OK

I am excited about _____

_____

_____ .

Daily Gratitude Journal for Kids

Circle one

Mon   Tue   Wed   Thurs   Fri   Sat   Sun

Month _____   Day ____   Year _____

I am thankful for _____ because

_____ .

I am also thankful for _____ because

_____ .

Draw something that makes you happy.

Today will be:

 Super Awesome and Amazing

 Great

 Good

 Just OK

I am excited about _____

_____

_____ .

 # Circle one

Mon   Tue   Wed   Thurs   Fri   Sat   Sun

Month _____ Day ____ Year _____

I am thankful for _____ because

_____ .

I am also thankful for _____ because

_____ .

Draw something that makes you happy.

 Today will be:

 Super Awesome and Amazing

 Great

 Good

 Just OK

I am excited about _____

_____

_____ .

Daily Gratitude Journal for Kids

Circle one

Mon   Tue   Wed   Thurs   Fri   Sat   Sun

Month _____ Day ____ Year _____

I am thankful for _____ because
_____ .

I am also thankful for _____ because
_____ .

Draw something that makes you happy.

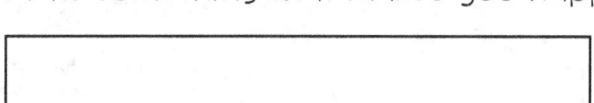

Today will be:

 Super Awesome and Amazing

 Great

 Good

 Just OK

I am excited about _____
_____
_____ .

Daily Gratitude Journal for Kids

 **Circle one**

Mon   Tue   Wed   Thurs   Fri   Sat   Sun

Month _____ Day ____ Year _____

I am thankful for _____ because
_____ .

I am also thankful for _____ because
_____ .

Draw something that makes you happy.

Today will be:
☆ Super Awesome and Amazing
☆ Great
☆ Good
☆ Just OK

I am excited about _____
_____
_____ .

Circle one

Mon   Tue   Wed   Thurs   Fri   Sat   Sun

Month _____   Day _____   Year _____

I am thankful for _____ because _____ .

I am also thankful for _____ because _____ .

Draw something that makes you happy.

Today will be:
- ☆ Super Awesome and Amazing
- ☆ Great
- ☆ Good
- ☆ Just OK

I am excited about _____ _____ _____ .

 **Circle one**

Mon   Tue   Wed   Thurs   Fri   Sat   Sun

Month _____ Day ____ Year _____

I am thankful for _____ because
_____ .

I am also thankful for _____ because
_____ .

Draw something that makes you happy.

Today will be:
☆ Super Awesome and Amazing
☆ Great
☆ Good
☆ Just OK

I am excited about _____
_____
_____ .

Circle one

Mon   Tue   Wed   Thurs   Fri   Sat   Sun

Month _____ Day ____ Year _____

I am thankful for _____ because _____ .

I am also thankful for _____ because _____ .

Draw something that makes you happy.

Today will be:
- ☆ Super Awesome and Amazing
- ☆ Great
- ☆ Good
- ☆ Just OK

I am excited about _____
_____
_____ .

Circle one

Mon   Tue   Wed   Thurs   Fri   Sat   Sun

Month _____ Day ____ Year _____

I am thankful for _____ because
_____ .

I am also thankful for _____ because
_____ .

Draw something that makes you happy.

Today will be:
☆ Super Awesome and Amazing
☆ Great
☆ Good
☆ Just OK

I am excited about _____
_____
_____ .

86   Daily Gratitude Journal for Kids

Circle one

Mon　　Tue　　Wed　　Thurs　　Fri　　Sat　　Sun

Month _____ Day _____ Year _____

I am thankful for _____ because

_____ .

I am also thankful for _____ because

_____ .

Draw something that makes you happy.

Today will be:

 Super Awesome and Amazing

 Great

 Good

 Just OK

I am excited about _____

_____

_____ .

Daily Gratitude Journal for Kids

 **Circle one**

Mon   Tue   Wed   Thurs   Fri   Sat   Sun

Month _____   Day ____   Year _____

I am thankful for _____ because

_____ .

I am also thankful for _____ because

_____ .

Draw something that makes you happy.

Today will be:
 Super Awesome and Amazing
 Great
 Good
 Just OK

I am excited about _____

_____

_____ .

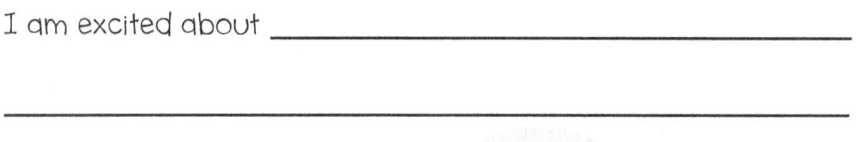

Daily Gratitude Journal for Kids

Circle one

Mon   Tue   Wed   Thurs   Fri   Sat   Sun

Month _____ Day ____ Year _____

I am thankful for _____ because
_____ .

I am also thankful for _____ because
_____ .

Draw something that makes you happy.

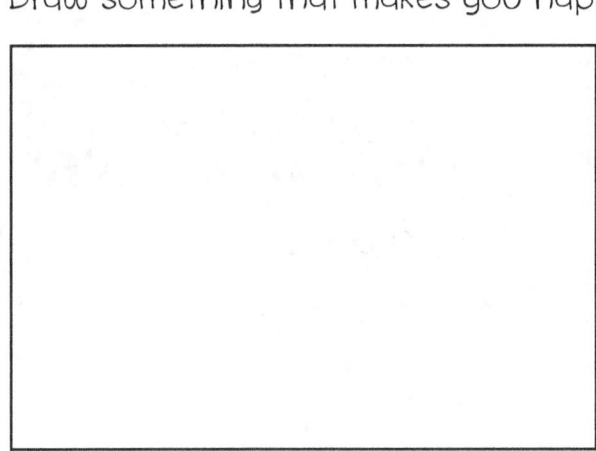

Today will be:

 Super Awesome and Amazing

 Great

 Good

 Just OK

I am excited about _____
_____
_____ .

Daily Gratitude Journal for Kids

 **Circle one**

Mon   Tue   Wed   Thurs   Fri   Sat   Sun

Month _____   Day _____   Year _____

I am thankful for _____ because
_____ .

I am also thankful for _____ because
_____ .

Draw something that makes you happy.

Today will be:
☆ Super Awesome and Amazing
☆ Great
☆ Good
☆ Just OK

I am excited about _____
_____
_____

 **Circle one**

Mon   Tue   Wed   Thurs   Fri   Sat   Sun

Month _____   Day ____   Year _____

I am thankful for _____ because
_____ .

I am also thankful for _____ because
_____ .

Draw something that makes you happy.

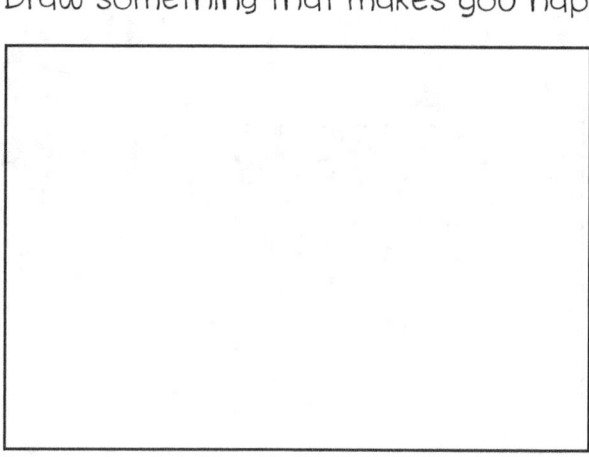

Today will be:

 Super Awesome and Amazing

 Great

 Good

 Just OK

I am excited about _____
_____
_____

Circle one

Mon   Tue   Wed   Thurs   Fri   Sat   Sun

Month _____   Day ____   Year _____

I am thankful for _____ because

_____ .

I am also thankful for _____ because

_____ .

Draw something that makes you happy.

Today will be:
☆ Super Awesome and Amazing
☆ Great
☆ Good
☆ Just OK

I am excited about _____

_____

_____ .

Circle one

Mon   Tue   Wed   Thurs   Fri   Sat   Sun

Month _____   Day ____   Year _____

I am thankful for _____ because
_____ .

I am also thankful for _____ because
_____ .

Draw something that makes you happy.

Today will be:

 Super Awesome and Amazing

 Great

 Good

 Just OK

I am excited about _____
_____
_____ .

Daily Gratitude Journal for Kids

Circle one

Mon   Tue   Wed   Thurs   Fri   Sat   Sun

Month _____   Day ____   Year _____

I am thankful for _____ because
_____ .

I am also thankful for _____ because
_____ .

Draw something that makes you happy.

Today will be:
☆ Super Awesome and Amazing
☆ Great
☆ Good
☆ Just OK

I am excited about _____
_____
_____ .

Circle one

Mon   Tue   Wed   Thurs   Fri   Sat   Sun

Month _____ Day ____ Year _____

I am thankful for _____ because
_____ .

I am also thankful for _____ because
_____ .

Draw something that makes you happy.

Today will be:
☆ Super Awesome and Amazing
☆ Great
☆ Good
☆ Just OK

I am excited about _____
_____
_____ .

Circle one

Mon   Tue   Wed   Thurs   Fri   Sat   Sun

Month _____   Day ____   Year _____

I am thankful for _____ because
_____ .

I am also thankful for _____ because
_____ .

Draw something that makes you happy.

Today will be:
☆ Super Awesome and Amazing
☆ Great
☆ Good
☆ Just OK

I am excited about _____
_____
_____ .

Circle one

Mon   Tue   Wed   Thurs   Fri   Sat   Sun

Month _____   Day ____   Year _____

I am thankful for _____ because

_____ .

I am also thankful for _____ because

_____ .

Draw something that makes you happy.

Today will be:
- ☆ Super Awesome and Amazing
- ☆ Great
- ☆ Good
- ☆ Just OK

I am excited about _____

_____

_____ .

Circle one

Mon   Tue   Wed   Thurs   Fri   Sat   Sun

Month _____   Day ____   Year _____

I am thankful for _____ because
_____ .

I am also thankful for _____ because
_____ .

Draw something that makes you happy.

Today will be:
☆ Super Awesome and Amazing
☆ Great
☆ Good
☆ Just Ok

I am excited about _____
_____
_____ .

Circle one

Mon   Tue   Wed   Thurs   Fri   Sat   Sun

Month _____ Day _____ Year _____

I am thankful for _____ because _____ .

I am also thankful for _____ because _____ .

Draw something that makes you happy.

Today will be:
- ☆ Super Awesome and Amazing
- ☆ Great
- ☆ Good
- ☆ Just OK

I am excited about _____
_____
_____ .

Circle one

Mon   Tue   Wed   Thurs   Fri   Sat   Sun

Month _____   Day ____   Year _____

I am thankful for _____ because

_____ .

I am also thankful for _____ because

_____ .

Draw something that makes you happy.

Today will be:
☆ Super Awesome and Amazing
☆ Great
☆ Good
☆ Just OK

I am excited about _____

_____

_____ .

Thank You!

I hope you enjoyed your 100 days of gratitude journey!

Please continue your gratitude journey and have your parents or guardians email us if you we can help or you have a success story to share!
Gratitude@CreativeIdeasPublishing.com

Discover more Titles from Creative Ideas Publishing

 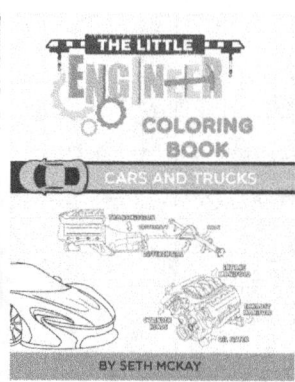  

 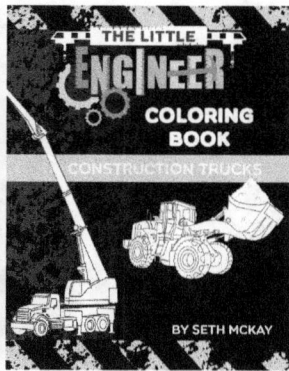  

www.ingramcontent.com/pod-product-compliance
Lightning Source LLC
Chambersburg PA
CBHW081753100526
44592CB00015B/2414